WITHDRAWN

SOUTHWESTERN STUDIES

MONOGRAPH No. 30

/\/\/\/\/\/\/\/\/\/\/\/\/\/\/\/\/\/\/\

Riders of the Border

A selection of thirty drawings

by

JOSÉ CISNEROS

with text by the artist

/\/\/\/\/\/\/\/\/\/\/\/\/\/\/\/\/\/\/\

ABOUT THE ARTIST

JOSÉ CISNEROS came to El Paso del Norte at the age of fifteen and lived in Juarez from 1925 until 1934, at which time he moved his residence to El Paso, where he became a U. S. citizen in 1948. Although some of his early drawings had been published in Mexico City and Juarez, his art career really began in 1937 when he took some drawings to the Federal Courthouse in El Paso, where Tom Lea was working on a mural. Lea looked at the drawings, recognized Cisneros' talent, and introduced him to Carl Hertzog, the printer who was beginning to publish books. Hertzog asked Cisneros to make some illustrations, including maps which Cisneros does with excellent calligraphic lettering and appropriate decoration. Thus began an association which extended over thirty-five years and resulted in dozens of books. Cisneros, who was born April 18, 1910 in the Mexican state of Durango, obtained his only formal education at Lydia Patterson Institute in El Paso. His knowledge of art and history has been acquired through his reading, research, and correspondence with other artists and scholars. He has illustrated (in total or in part) over forty books, most of which deal with the Southwest. In 1969, Cisneros was the fourth recipient of a residence fellowship given by The University of Texas. He spent six months at J. Frank Dobie's Paisano Ranch, where he completed several of the drawings in this *Southwestern Study*. His "riders" project is one which has occupied Cisneros for many years and one which grows larger and more popular as the drawings are exhibited throughout the country, where five showings are scheduled during 1971. The artist resides in El Paso at 3703 Hueco with his wife, Vicenta, and three of their five daughters.

—E. H. A.

RIDERS OF THE BORDER

by José Cisneros

THIS IS A PICTURE BOOK in which I have been concerned with the appearance, the picturesqueness, the pageantry of the characters depicted rather than with the technicalities of horsemanship or the scholarly accuracy of assertions; therefore, if mistakes exist, they are mine. To those who enjoy the æsthetic qualities of the renderings, I acknowledge grateful appreciation; to the learned and erudite who detect an error, I ask indulgence and understanding.

To the many friends who have meant so much in the preparation of this little volume, I express gratitude and esteem. Special mention should be made of the following: Joseph Hefter of Mexico City from whom I received so abundantly and so generously; E. Haywood Antone of the Texas Western Press for his involvement in printing this book and for his assistance in editing my notes; Tom Lea of El Paso for his perennial advice and timely counsel; Dr. Paul A. Rossi of the Gilcrease Institute of American Art and History, Tulsa, Oklahoma; Dr. Arthur Woodward, University of Arizona, Tucson; Dr. Ray Billington, Huntington Library, San Marino, California; August W. Sachtra, L. A. Westerners Corral, San Marino; L. Henderson Shuffler and Al Lowman, Institute of Texan Cultures, San Antonio; Frank H. Wardlaw, University of Texas Press, Austin; Dr. Joe B. Frantz and Dr. L. Tuffly Ellis, Texas State Historical Association, Austin; Dr. John Porter Bloom, National Archives, Washington, D. C.; Dr. Sandra L. Myres, The University of Texas at Arlington; Mrs. Sheila Ohlendorf, Hall of the Horseman, Humanities Research Center, University of Texas at Austin; Henry Schipman, Jr., Las Cruces, New Mexico; Mrs. J. Frank Dobie of Austin; Randy Steffen of Fort Pierce, Florida—all have provided me with assistance, interviews, photographs, books, and picture material. My thanks go also to my wife, Vicenta, for tender care, silence and patience when I needed them most, and to Vivian and Carl Hertzog, for the treasure of their friendship and their unwavering faith throughout our vigils.

El Paso, Texas
May 17, 1971

SPANISH *CONQUISTADOR*

Early 16th Century

THE SPANISH DOMINATION of the Western hemisphere and the expansion of their frontier began with the landing of Cortés at Vera Cruz, April 19, 1519. The first horses—sixteen in number—arrived with this expedition. Soldiers who were fortunate enough to have a horse still faced the problem of limited equipment they were able to gather in the ill supplied and distant inland settlements. A horse soldier at the time of the Conquest of Mexico must have been equipped with odd and outdated pieces of armor, a salade for a head covering, a breastplate, sword, dagger and lance, probably a coat of mail and the ever present *adarga,* which were oval shields adapted from the Moors and were made of stiff leather; therefore, they were rather light and tough. Swords usually came from the forges of Toledo. Firearms were few and reserved for very special occasions. Jingle bells were attached to the breast and croup straps of the saddles to impress the natives and create turmoil among them.

SPANISH SOLDIER

Middle 16th Century

MILITARY UNIFORM as a fixed form of dress officially
prescribed and regulated was not known in the Sixteenth Century. Soldiers could be distinguished from
civilians by the offensive and defensive equipment
which they wore in the discharge of their duties. In the
Spanish colonies, as well as in most European coun-
tries, it was a common sight to see soldiers wearing the
same type of garments as the town-folk with the exception of their weapons and armor.

The rider is wearing a soft velvet cap, cuirass, and
soft leather heeless boots. Heels did not appear in the
new lands until the beginning of the Seventeenth Century. A curious fact is that boots and shoes at that time
were manufactured without any difference between the
right and left foot and were worn indiscriminately.

SPANISH CAPTAIN GENERAL

1590

WITH THE DISCOVERY OF SILVER MINES, the great increase in livestock, the extensive land grants, expanded trade, and abundant cheap labor, wealth came easily and rapidly to the nobility and to those whom the Crown favored.

Luxury and ostentation in dress became so rampant in the new lands that the Spanish Court issued laws and ordinances prohibiting the excessive display of expensive and extravagant garments. For the most part these laws and regulations were ignored or flagrantly disobeyed.

Our drawing depicts an army officer in the richly embroidered and ornamented dress of the period. His headpiece is the type of salade known as *borgonota.* His short cape is a *ferreruelo.* The rump housing of the saddle received the name of *gualdrapa* and its use was reserved for the nobility and high ranking officers. Years later Mexican rural horsemen began to make to their saddles a leather adaption of these trappings culminating in time with a full, ornamented covering for the rear of the horse, naming it *anquera.*

J CISNEROS
EL PASO

THE VICEROY

Late 16th Century

KING PHILIP II, afflicted with a deep religious senti-
ment and a somber disposition, introduced into his
court the austerity of his convictions by denying his gay
and fun loving subjects the pleasure of wearing any-
thing but black clothing. The impact of his dictatorial
desires was so far reaching that scores of years after
his death, black remained the predominant color among
government officials in Spain as in the distant colonies.

The Viceroy is following the fashion dictates of the
Peninsula. He wears a ruffle around his neck known in
Spain as *gorguera*. It is said that at this time ruffles
became so large and unwieldy that an underprop was
devised to lift them up. His hat, perhaps a forerunner
of our tall silk hats, was originally named *a la Felipe
II*. His richly caparisoned horse reflects the wealth pre-
vailing in the land. His page or herald is wearing a
tabard with the embroidered royal arms of the dwind-
ling empire.

J. CISNEROS-68

SPANISH PIONEER WOMAN

c. 1650

IN THE ACCOUNT of the Oñate expedition to New Mexico in 1598, the writer mentions the great difficulties encountered along the way, across the great desert expanses. Especially arduous was the driving and handling of the great number of cattle, sheep and pigs. The journey was hard on the many brave Spanish women and their children. Even though they suffered the same privations in subsequent expeditions, the women continued to accompany their men. Typical of the courageous Spanish pioneer is the lady riding sideways on a mare with a pack saddle for a seat, a few dangling belongings and a young baby on her lap. She made the journey to carry on and fulfill the wishes of her king and to extend his borderlands.

CATTLE COMING INTO TEXAS

1690

WHEREVER THE SPANISH went to extend their frontier, whether to establish a settlement, a mission, a mining town, or a military outpost, they took their cattle and horses, their sheep and goats, even their chickens with them. Much of the success of their enterprises depended on an ample supply of livestock, which was the backbone of their economy.

The first colonizing expedition into Texas, headed by Captain Alonso de León came in 1690. Soldiers and missionaries handled the first herd ever to enter what became the Lone Star State. For the protection of both settlers and the herds, soldiers performed the role of herd driver.

Our man leading the group carries a cuirass—breast and back plates. His loose and baggy pants were known as *zahones* and were used in Spain before and after the conquest of Mexico. Indeed, they are still used in some provinces as part of the typical attire. The saddle is one of the earliest types of *sillas vaqueras* — cowboy saddles. The horn has a metal ring around the head to reinforce it. The leather covering was known as *mochila;* the stirrups show Moorish decendency. The rider holds a hocking tool called *media luna* or *desjarretadera* and a rawhide waterbag hangs from the saddle horn.

FRONTIERSMAN

1700

FATHER EUSEBIO FRANCISCO KINO had a very special place in the exploration and settlement of the West. With good reason, the State of Arizona declared him an outstanding son. He was a missionary, man of science and letters, geographer, explorer, builder, stockman. In addition to all this, he was an extraordinary horseman.

To him belongs the honor for the first Spanish settlements in the *Pimería Alta,* as Arizona was then known. Along with the many missions that he founded, he created breeding centers of livestock that accounted for thousands of animals. The work which Father Kino did as a ranchman alone would stamp him as unusual business man. As an example of the success of his enterprises, he mentioned that Mission San Xavier del Bac (near Tucson) was started with seven hundred heads of cattle from the herds of Mission Dolores. He transformed the wild, newly converted Indians from nomads to self-supporting people. The modern stock raising industry is endebted on a considerable scale to this indefatigable man. He felt great fascination for all kind of livestock, cattle, horses, mules, goats and sheep and was extremely proud of the two huge sheepskins on which he used to sleep because they had been selected from rams of his own corrals.

His deeds and performances on horseback were incredible. In 1695, at fifty years of age, he made a trip from Mission Dolores to Mexico City (roughly seventeen hundred miles) in fifty-three days on horseback. His constant visits to his missions and cattle establishments resulted in daily rides of approximately twenty miles. He was indeed a remarkable and practical frontiersman who carried the cross in one hand and the branding iron in the other.

TEXAS FRANCISCAN MISSIONARY

1750

THE FOOTPRINTS OF THE FRANCISCANS can be detected today across our Spanish Southwest, from Matagorda Bay to Cape Mendocino, from Sierra Nevada to Paso del Norte. They marked their path with institutions, monuments, traditions, and customs that have remained through the centuries. In their journeys, the Franciscans followed Estéban the Moor and Francisco Vásquez Coronado; they were with Antonio de Espejo and with the Adelantado don Juan de Oñate. They traversed the land with the soldiers and without them. Sometimes they were protected by the military; other times they were left to their own resources.

No group of men had more influence in the founding of the pivotal cities of the Spanish borderlands than the members of the Order of Friars Minors. San Francisco, San Antonio, San Diego, Los Angeles, Santa Fe, Guadalupe de El Paso del Norte—all attest and proclaim with their sonorous Spanish names the Franciscan heritage of their origin.

Junípero Serra, Marcos de Niza, Francisco Garcés, Antonio de Jesús Margil, Agustín Rodriguez, Alonso de Benavides, García de San Francisco are a few in the long and illustrious roster of great benefactors of the Southwest. Their names are intimately united with the history, traditions and development of our land and they should be remembered forever.

Although in their establishments the Franciscans were surrounded with cattle, horses and mules, the statutes of their Order and their triple religious vow of poverty, chastity and obedience prevented them from riding horses, except on very extraordinary circumstances.

J. CISNEROS
PAISANO

LANCER OF THE GULF COAST

1770

WHILE THE "CUERA" DRAGOONS were operating along the northern Mexico line of *presidios* across our present Southwest from the Pacific to the Gulf of Mexico, another group of soldiers, just as picturesque, guarded the eastern approaches to New Spain. They operated from Vera Cruz to what is now Brownsville, Texas. They were officially known as *Lanceros de Vera Cruz*.

Their uniforms consisted of a tight fitting buckskin jacket with puffed and slashed short sleeves, reminiscent or perhaps a hangover of those worn in the late sixteenth century. A wide and beautifully embossed bandolier served as both a pistol and sword holder. The short sword had the appearance of a *machete*—sugar cane cutting knife. The saddle was of the *jineta* type, with heavy cross stirrups, the kind that have puzzled Mexican historians concerning their use. The rider is wearing a native regional straw hat suitable for the tropical climate. The drawing is based on a contemporary watercolor found and shared by Joseph Hefter, internationally known military historian, outstanding artist and translator, and friend of the artist.

J CISNEROS
EL PASO

DRAGOON 2nd CO, SAN LUIS MILITIA

1779

LATE IN THE SEVENTEENTH CENTURY the different commercial trade and handcrafts guilds of Mexico City began to show displeasure and opposition to the Flemish troops in the service of Spain and to their extravagant Walloon uniforms by organizing and maintaining, at their own expense, armed and uniformed companies of militia to replace the Flemish troops in the defense of towns and harbors. Once the Dragoons were established in Mexico City, other cities followed the example and organized their own. The custom prevailed throughout the country for more than a century. Each company adopted its own particular uniform designed accordingly to the contemporary military fashion trends. Most of them were dressed at great expense, displaying costly fabrics as well as gold and silver embroideries which caused the envy of the regular soldier clad in a relatively modest manner.

The Dragoon is wearing a uniform similar in cut as that of the regular army. Coat, vest and cockade were red; lapels, cuffs, lining, breeches, saddlecloth and holster covers are blue; lace and buttons are yellow. Dragoons wore cloth leggings with buckles instead of boots.

CALIFORNIA *CUERA* DRAGOON

1790

ONE OF THE MOST PECULIAR and picturesque group of soldiers that ever trod the Southwest were the "Cuera" Dragoons of Spain. A very singular and interesting feature of their uniforms was the leather, buckskin or sometimes rawhide, coat they wore and from which they acquired their nickname. It was padded with six or seven layers of rawhide to make it arrowproof. It had evolved through the centuries from the quilted cotton armor of the Aztecs and hispanized *escaupil*. This cotton armor had proved to be such an excellent protection that it had been adopted by the conquistadores.

The picture is based on a drawing in the Naval Museum in Madrid made by José Cardero, an artist member of the Alejandro Malaspina expedition that visited Monterey, California in 1791. The saddle is a type originally brought from Mexico through Baja California where it still is used with a few modifications.

SPANISH OFFICER OF THE FRONTIER

1790

AMONG THE SPANISH FRONTIERSMEN of the second
half of the eighteenth century, Juan Bautista de Anza,
Felipe de Neve, Juan de Ugalde and Hugo O'Conor
stand out as four of the greatest. Considering the vast-
ness, the emptiness and dryness of our Southwestern
deserts one wonders about the hardships, labors and
disappointments those men had to face and endure.
No one knows how many were lost, were victims of
hunger and thirst, or were killed by the resentful natives.

Typical of this period is the officer in our drawing.
The difficulties of his journeys show in his tattered
uniform, his torn and patched equipment, his face un-
shaven but showing great determination in the fulfill-
ment of his commission.

SPANISH MEXICAN *HACENDADO*

1750

FROM THE SCATTERED GRAPHIC MATERIAL of the mid-eighteenth Century in Mexico (paintings, engravings, drawings, watercolors, tiles) we tried to make a reconstruction of the appearance of a wealthy Creole *hacendado* of the period.

The round, closed, short cape he is wearing seems to have been the origin of the *manga*—a garment that was already being used at this time, displayed by many rich *rancheros*. The *manga* was a circular ankle-length cape with an opening in the center for the head. The opening had an extra piece of cloth of different color; it extended around the shoulders and was richly decorated with gold fringe along the edge.

The breeches were knee length and already showed incipient ornamentation that later would become the row of silver buttons characteristic of the Mexican horseman's pantaloons.

His foot gear was a development of previous European fashionable styles in shoes. This also in time evolved into other types of footwear, popular among country people at the beginning of the Nineteenth Century.

INDIAN MISSION *VAQUERO*

1800

"INDIANS, EVEN IF DESCENDANT from kings, are not allowed to ride horses, under penalty of death." Thus, a Spanish mandate was directed against the naturals of New Spain, forbidding their use of horses. Although the Spaniards were very severe in enforcing these laws, there were many times in which the Indians either secretly or through the help of others found the way or occasion to get on a horse.

In the missions of the Southwest, especially in California, some of the *padres* were not only extraordinarily good teachers but also excellent horsemen. Due to the increasing size of their herds and the work that resulted, the *padres* diligently taught the neophytes the essentials of horsemanship. Those early vaquero candidates experienced many hard spills before they qualified and, one might say, they really earned their spurs.

SPANISH TEXAS FIELD JUDGE

c. 1805

A SPANIARD OF THE FRONTIER known only to a few historians who delve into the forgotten and dusty archives of yesteryear was the *juez de campo* — field judge. "He functioned as an itinerant judge charged with investigating thefts, robberies, carrying away of properties by force, burning of houses, grain or other things, whenever the said crimes may be committed in unsettled districts . . . . He was also responsible for keeping all records concerning livestock such as the names of stockmen, location of ranches and records of brand registrations," according to Professor Sandra L. Myres in *The Ranch in Spanish Texas* (El Paso: Texas Western Press, 1969).

At the rodeos he would display his importance signaling and shaking his baton—a reglementary sign of authority—so the *rancheros* big and small might divide their stock from that owned by the missions.

J. CISNEROS
EL PASO

MEXICAN LANCER

1839

FROM THE FIRST DAY of its independence, Mexico faced difficulty in organizing and reconstructing her governmental structure because of internal strifes, dissensions, quarrels and competition for power. This state of affairs plagued the country for decades, weakening it and making it an easy target for expanding and ambitious nations. Her disorganized, but stoic and patriotic soldiers conducted themselves bravely and as fiercely when compelled to face, at different times, the armies of Spain, France, the United States and the newly created Republic of Texas.

Different governments gave different orders and dispositions during the 1830's and 1840's for the creation of a variety of uniforms. The Lancer is representative of the varied color combinations of the period. He belongs to the 8th Cavalry Regiment and his uniform consisted of Turkish blue tailcoat and pants, deep red lapels and cuffs, white collar and cuff bars, and green saddle blanket.

J. CISNEROS
EL PASO

MEXICAN *RANCHERO*

1840

THE PICTURESQUENESS, the pageantry, the æsthetic appeal of the Mexican riding dress is exemplified by the variety of styles prevalent in the middle of the 1800's. Fortunately, traveling artists who visited Mexico at that period (Carl Nebel, Johann Moritz Rugendas, and Thomas Egerton) left valuable documentary evidence of their observations. Also a very significant contemporary witness was Madame Calderón de la Barca, who left lively descriptions in her book, *Life in Mexico.*

Our rendering is based on a group of accurately done small wax figures that Madame Calderón mentions and which are still extant at the Museo de América in Madrid. The garment over his shoulder is similar to the *manga* except that it is open like a cape and is known as *ruana* or *ruano.* Other coverings were the *sarape* and the *manta* or *jorongo,* which in reality was a *sarape* with an opening for the head in the center. A *poncho* is a South American version of the same garment. His leggings *(botas de ala)* were wrapped around towards the front, giving the appearance of wider pants *(pantaloneras).* The short, slip-on jacket with epaulettes *(cotona)* was common in these years.

J. CISNEROS
EL PASO

MEXICAN MULETEER

Early 19th Century

TRAPPERS AND MOUNTAIN men who wandered into the Southwest returned to the Mississippi River towns, where they often incited the greed and curiosity of their listeners by exclaiming, "Those Spaniards at Santa Fe have more gold and silver than a dog's got fleas, but no place to spend it!" Such provocative chatter often resulted in thoughts of how Americans could profit by sending wagon loads of goods cheaper, better, and faster than could the Spanish merchants from Mexico.

The reported accumulated wealth of New Mexicans was the result of lack of commerce in the province. Since early times, their trade had depended on the very irregular and hazardous trips made by the ox-cart caravans and mule back trains from Mexico to Santa Fe.

Usually these pack trains consisted of four or five hundred mules and approximately seventy-five muleteers on foot *(arrieros)*. Every day, each driver had to gather the animals assigned to him, load them, stay along with them, and remove the pack at the end of the day's journey. There were some who took care of the spare animals *(remudas)* and who provided supplies and water for the group as well as feed for the beasts during the rest periods. Two items essential to the muleteer were the *pechera,* a leather apron, and the *tapojo,* a piece of buckskin with long thongs attached that served the double purpose of blindfold and whip. Because the mules were sensitive and easily scared, they had to be blindfolded everytime they were loaded and unloaded. If the pack needed adjusting along the trail, the operation was repeated.

J. CISNEROS-64

CALIFORNIA *CABALLERO*

1840

IN THE WORDS OF BANCROFT, who gathered the most accurate information concerning early California, nothing was more important to the Caballero than the trappings of his horse. With an ideal environment, the Caballero's greatest preocupation was to maintain excellent horses and the finest of attire and riding equipment.

When he rode horseback, he wore his legs enveloped in beautifully decorated leggings called *gamuzas*. Of these, he was very proud, and his method of wrapping his leg was an art in itself. A mantle was worn in cold weather and consisted of a piece of woolen cloth with an opening for the head, similar, except that it was shorter, to the one used in Mexico. This garment had both grace and dignity and also allowed great freedom of movement.

Born to the saddle, gay in his trappings, fearless in horsemanship, the *caballero* was one of the most dashing riders the world has ever seen.

J. CISNEROS
PAISANO

TEXAS HERDSMAN

1858

FROM A REPRINT of a story in Frank Leslie's *Illustrated Newspaper,* January 15, 1859, we gathered the material to reconstruct what the English-speaking people of the time termed a "herdsman," referring to the Mexican cowboys at the service of land-holding Anglo settlers in Texas.

It was natural in a rural society which for generations had depended on cattle for its subsistence, that the livestock industry should become the main occupation.

A slanted and biased view of this situation is given by the reporter (one Richard Everett) in his article. Displaying arrogance and racial discrimination, he stated, "A large element of the population of San Antonio is Mexican. There are a few respectable, intelligent and wealthy families but the majority are of the lower order, with all the vices and none of the virtues belonging to the better situated. The men, whenever they work, are employed as teamsters, *herdsmen* and day laborers. It is general belief, founded I believe, on fact, that a Mexican is good for nothing unless in service over cattle, horses and mules. The bend of their talents is toward livestock."

TEXAS RANGER

1870

THE MOST FAMOUS ORGANIZATION of frontier fighters for law and order in the Southwest was undoubtedly the Texas Rangers. The Rangers were named "a special body of irregular troops." As such they were set apart from the regular Army of Texas, as well as from her volunteer militia. Although subjected to military discipline, the Ranger carried no flag, wore no badge, no insignia or rank, no official uniform. He had to furnish his own weapons and mount. He never killed a man he did not have to kill, but he had to kill many men, his exalters declare, making him the good guy in his fight with his traditional foes — Indians, Anglo troublemakers and Mexicans. In most accounts, he usually appears as the winner, whether the odds were three to one, eight to one or even a dozen to one.

J. CISNEROS
PAISANO

BUFFALO SOLDIER

1880

THE ARMY THAT EMERGED from the Civil War tamed the last frontiers of the Southwest and became the frontier army of the West. Postwar Indian combat and exploration kept the soldiers active. Protecting the establishment of new settlements, guarding the building of railroads, watching trails and communications were a few of the functions the army had to perform. New forts were created as bases for supplies and operations. Fort Stockton, Fort Quitman and particularly Fort Davis in the Big Bend region were garrisoned by the colorful "Buffalo Soldiers" as the Negro troops in those places became known.

Many of the white officers in command of these soldiers made no secret of their contempt towards them. Discrimination ran rampant; supplies, equipment, quarters and assignments were often detoured or withheld. In spite of humiliations and unfair treatment, these enduring soldiers compiled outstanding records of service in action.

For several years the 9th and 10th Cavalry as well as the 24th and 25th Infantry, composed of black soldiers, added the striking appearance of their uniforms to the desert landscape. Ironically, they were engaged in the pursuit and extermination of other minorities who did not willingly relinquish their freedom or their rights.

SOUTH TEXAS COWBOY

1880

SCORES OF EXPERTS have given various opinions concerning the origin and the development of the American cowboy. Almost everything that can be said about him has been told and retold. The amount of literature devoted to him surpasses that devoted to any other frontier character. His image has been reproduced, along with that of his inseparable equine companion, by the great, the near great and by unknowns. His deeds and his doings have been recorded in all media. His lingo, his songs, his sayings, his mannerisms, his equipment, everything about him has been subjected to the analysis of the pens of generations of writers long gone, and no doubt will be re-analysed by those who are to come. His place in Western history is permanent and paramount.

We limit ourselves to give our personal impression of a good, old, down-to-earth South Texas cowboy of the 1880's.

MEXICAN *CHARRO*

1890

THE MEXICAN vaquero (the *charro*) has not fared as
well in art, history and literature as his counterpart in
the United States, the American cowboy. While the
cowboy has been depicted in detail, the history of the
hombre from the South and his four hundred years in
the saddle remains to be uncovered. Despite Mexico's
long equestrian tradition, the country has produced only a handful of men who have investigated, recorded, or
depicted the history and activities of its men on horseback. The *charros* have not had as their depicters such
men as Russell, Remington, James, Eggenhofer and Jo
Mora.

The drawing shows a *charro* at the turn of the last
century, when the *charros* still practiced their skill as
a profession rather than as a sport.

CHIHUAHUA *RANCHERO*

1905

To MANY PEOPLE, the physical appearance of Mexican country people seems monotonous and uniform. That is to say, once you have seen one, you have seen them all.

With a little insight, study and appreciation, one can see that the silhouette of the Mexican rider has changed through the years. The change is very apparent from decade to decade and from one region to another. With eyes peeled and a heart open, one can enjoy and appreciate the plastic qualities, the hidden attraction, and the simple and unspoiled beauty which the image of a Mexican horseman cuts on the clear horizon.

Characteristic of the northern *ranchero* from the states of Durango, Coahuila, and Chihuahua were the leather leggings known as *mitazas*. Some historians claim that they evolved from the buckskin leg coverings of the Apaches. A personal belief is that they are an adaptation in leather of similar pieces made of cloth worn by the regular Spanish soldiers of the frontier in the late 18th Century.

NORTHERN MEXICO REVOLUTIONARY

1914

`IN ESSENCE, THE MEXICAN REVOLUTION of 1914 was the clamor and protest of the rural population against the injustice of the government which supported a relatively small group of aristocrats while the peasantry was living in abject poverty and miserable conditions. This situation culminated in the armed revolt of the rural inhabitants, who demanded a change in their standard of living.

Those who joined the movement had to supply their own mounts and equipment. Our horseman represents a youngster following the troops and feeling the joy and attraction of his new adventure, with high dreams of a better tomorrow.

J. CISNEROS
EL PASO

SONORA *VAQUERO*

1950

MEXICO'S PECULIAR GEOGRAPHY is responsible in many ways for the differences in riding apparel in the many regions. Just as Baja California was isolated from the mainland by its gulf, the neighboring states of Sonora and Chihuahua remained separated in the past by the inaccessible Sierra Madres. Because these states were so close and yet so distant, the ornamental as well as the utilitarian parts of their saddles developed and evolved in quite different ways. The Sonoran *vaqueros* solved the problem of working and traveling through their thorny country by covering themselves and parts of their beasts in leather arranged in a very pleasing and decorative manner.

BAJA CALIFORNIA COWBOY

1960

THE NATURAL CONDITIONS of the terrain have kept the people from Baja California isolated from the rest of the country as well as from the United States. The natives have kept and retained many archaic customs and usages that in most places belong to history.

One of the peculiarities of Baja California is their riding equipment. They are using the same type of horse gear brought by their Spanish ancestors. They are a living link between their brother *vaqueros* across the Sea of Cortes and the American Cowboys.

The Baja horseman is literally wrapped in leather from his hat down to the tip of his saddle's *tapaderas*. He wears a knee-length buckskin coat belted with a long rawhide rope similar in many ways to the *cuera* of the Presidio soldiers in the late 18th Century. From knee to ankle, his legs are covered with stiff leather leggings *(polainas)*. With the exception of his fan-like leather aprons *(armas)* his saddle is a faithful recreation of those used in early-day California.

COLIMA RIDER

1970

TODAY, WHEN CEMENT AND ASPHALT are covering our countryside; when revolution, riots, new morality, smog and pollution are threatening; when the things that we believe in, the words that we say, the thoughts that we express do not convey the meaning we described to 'them yesteryear, it is a relief to escape and to find places where life is still unhurried, peaceful, uncontaminated by progress. One such place may be found, protected by nature and isolated by geography along the Southwest coast of Mexico. Today, one can see Colima horsemen riding through the twisting country roads of the volcanic region bordering the Mexican states of Jalisco, Michoacan and Colima. The horsemen are dressed in their native garb, with their polished round headed saddles and their peculiar palm leaf raincoats providing the appearance of a daguerrotype. Their saddles have a wide, unusual leather attachment (*armas*) on both sides, serving the purpose of chaps.

CHARRO

1970

DURING THE ALGID PERIOD of the Mexican revolution
(1910-1920) the traditionally *charro* costumes were re-
placed by Texas hats *(Tejanas)* and by canvas leggings
and the khaki riding trousers. During these terrible ten
years of internal struggle the principal *haciendas* were
destroyed, cattle killed or smuggled into the United
States and the entire nation came near ruin. And the
charros almost disappeared.

It was not until 1921, when Mexico celebrated its
first centennial of its political independence, that the
National Association of Charros was founded, princi-
pally through the efforts of a distinguished lawyer
from Tamaulipas named Ramon Cosío González. The
purpose of the association was to preserve, maintain
and guard the centuries-old equestrian traditions, costumes and customs of the rural livestock raising com-
munities. At first, members had difficulty finding prop-
er mounts and equipment. But as the years went by,
the national spirit awoke and today there are *charro*
associations all over Mexico and today these gentle-
men-riders are carrying on the way of life the traditions, and the horsemanship inherited from their illustrious predecessors.

SELECTED BIBLIOGRAPHY

Adams, Ramon F. *The Old-Time Cowhand*. New York, 1961.

Alvarez del Villar, Jose. *Historia de la Charreria*. Mexico, 1941.

Ainsworth, Ed. *The Cowboy in Art*. New York, 1968.

Cali, Francois. *The Spanish Arts of Latin America*. New York, 1960.

Carrillo y Gariel, Abelardo. *El Traje en la Nueva Espana*. Mexico, 1959.

Chenevix-Trench, Charles. *A History of Horsemanship*. New York, 1970.

Flores, Jesus Romero. *Iconografia Colonial*. Mexico, 1940.

Gomez de la Puente, Eusebio, ed. *Iconografia de Gobernantes de la Nueva Espana*. Mexico, 1921.

Gianoli, Luigi. *Horses and Horsemanship Through The Ages*. New York, 1969.

Hammond, George P. *Juan de Oñate and The Founding of New Mexico*. Albuquerque, 1927.

Hughes, Ann E. "The Beginnings of Spanish Settlement in the El Paso District," *University of California Publications in History*, I Berkeley, 1914.

Isenbart, Hans-Heinrich. *The Kingdom of the Horse*. Frankfort, 1969.

Mora, Jo. *Californios*. New York, 1949.

Mora, Jo. *Trail Dust and Saddle Leather*. New York, 1946.

Morris, George Ford. *Portraitures of Horses*. Shrewsbury, 1952.

Osborne, Walter D. and Patricia H. Johnson. *The Treasury of Horses*. New York, 1966.

Prescott, William H. *The Conquest of Mexico*. New York, 1843.

Romero de Terreros, Manuel. *Siluetas de Antaño*. Mexico, 1937.

Smith, Bradley. *The Horse in the West*. New York, 1969.

Tinker, Edward Larocque. *The Horseman of the Americas*. Austin, 1967.

Toussaint, Manuel. *Arte Colonial en Mexico*. Mexico, 1948.